Boo Gardens

Rebecca Demos

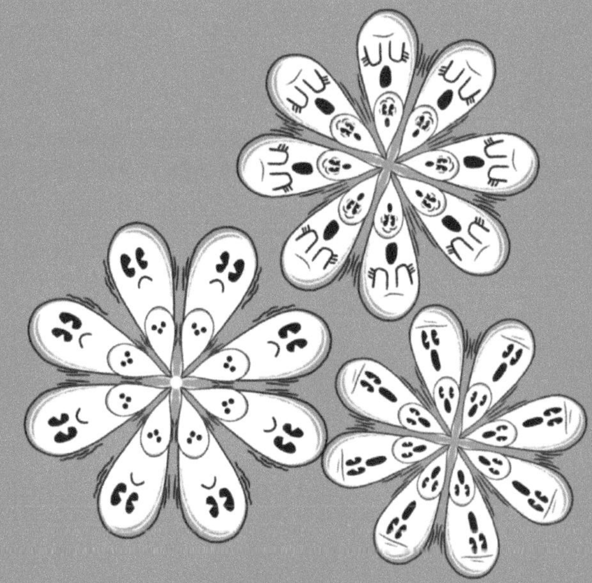

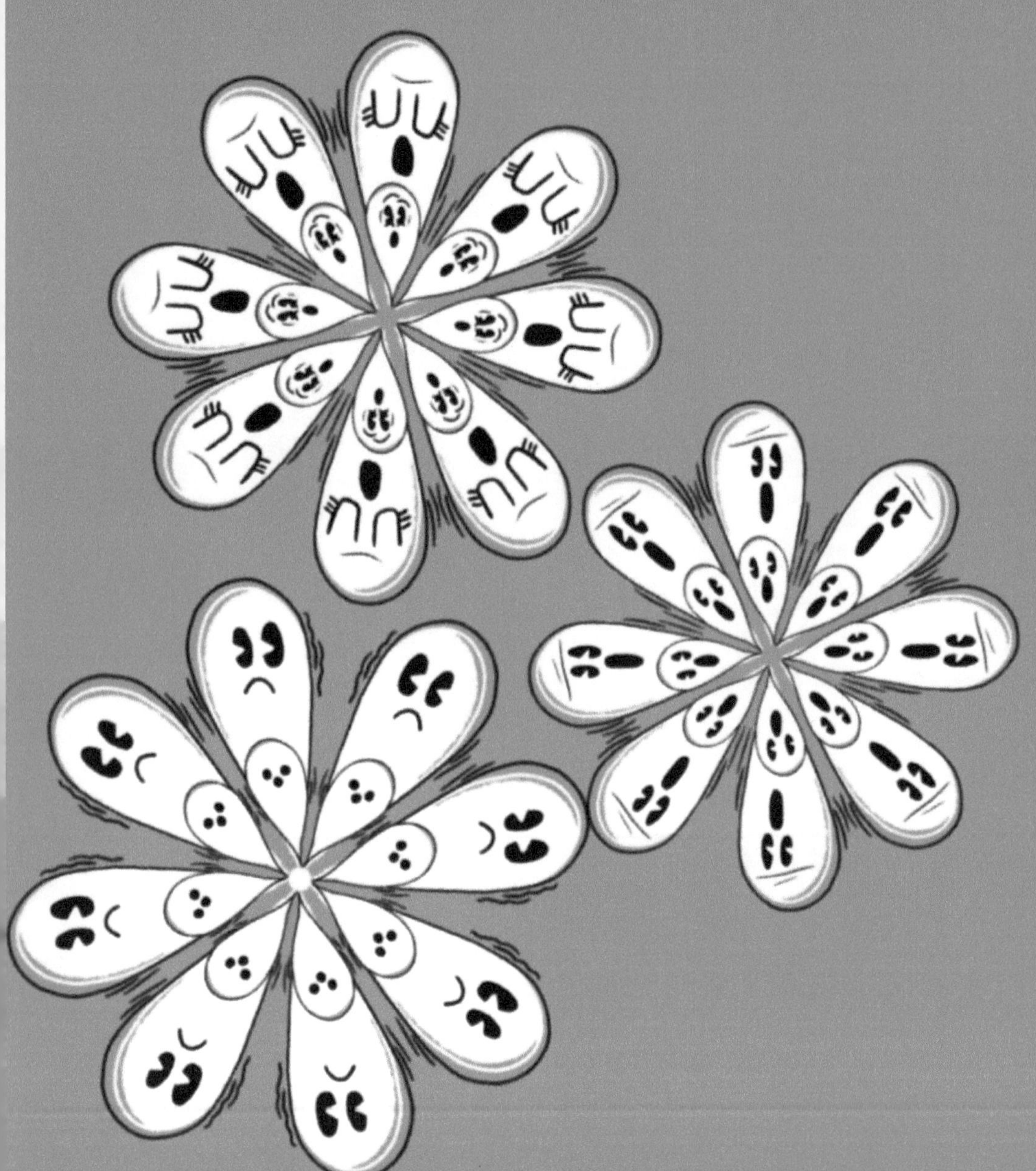

Boo Gardens
Text and illustrations Copyright 2023 by Rebecca Demos, all rights reserved.
Printed in the USA. No part of this book may be used or represented in any
manner whatsoever without expressed written permission except in the case of
brief quotations embodied in critical articles and reviews.
Book design by Rebecca Demos

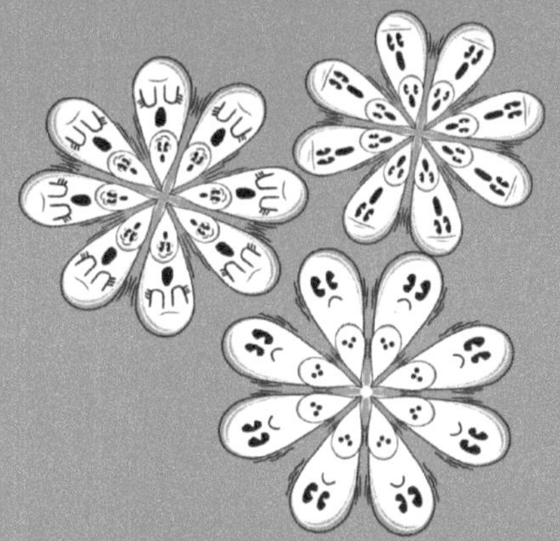

Let's draw spooky things.

This book belongs to

Black cats

or like this

Black cats

or like this

Sir. Purr

end

Pumpkins

Facial expressions

Mr. Pumpkin

start

end

Mr. & Mrs.

Spooky Silly Skulls

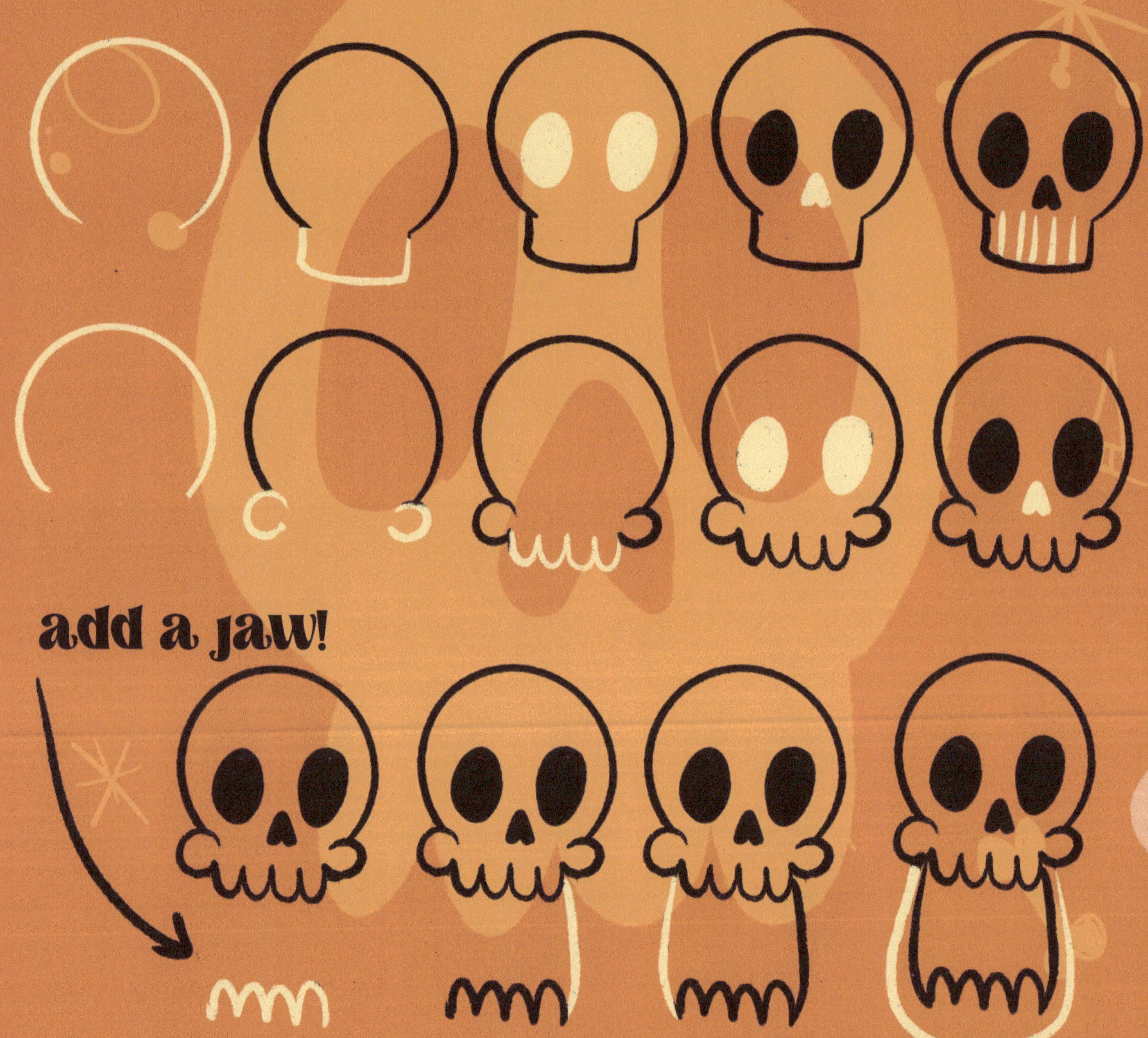

Spooky Silly Facial Expressions

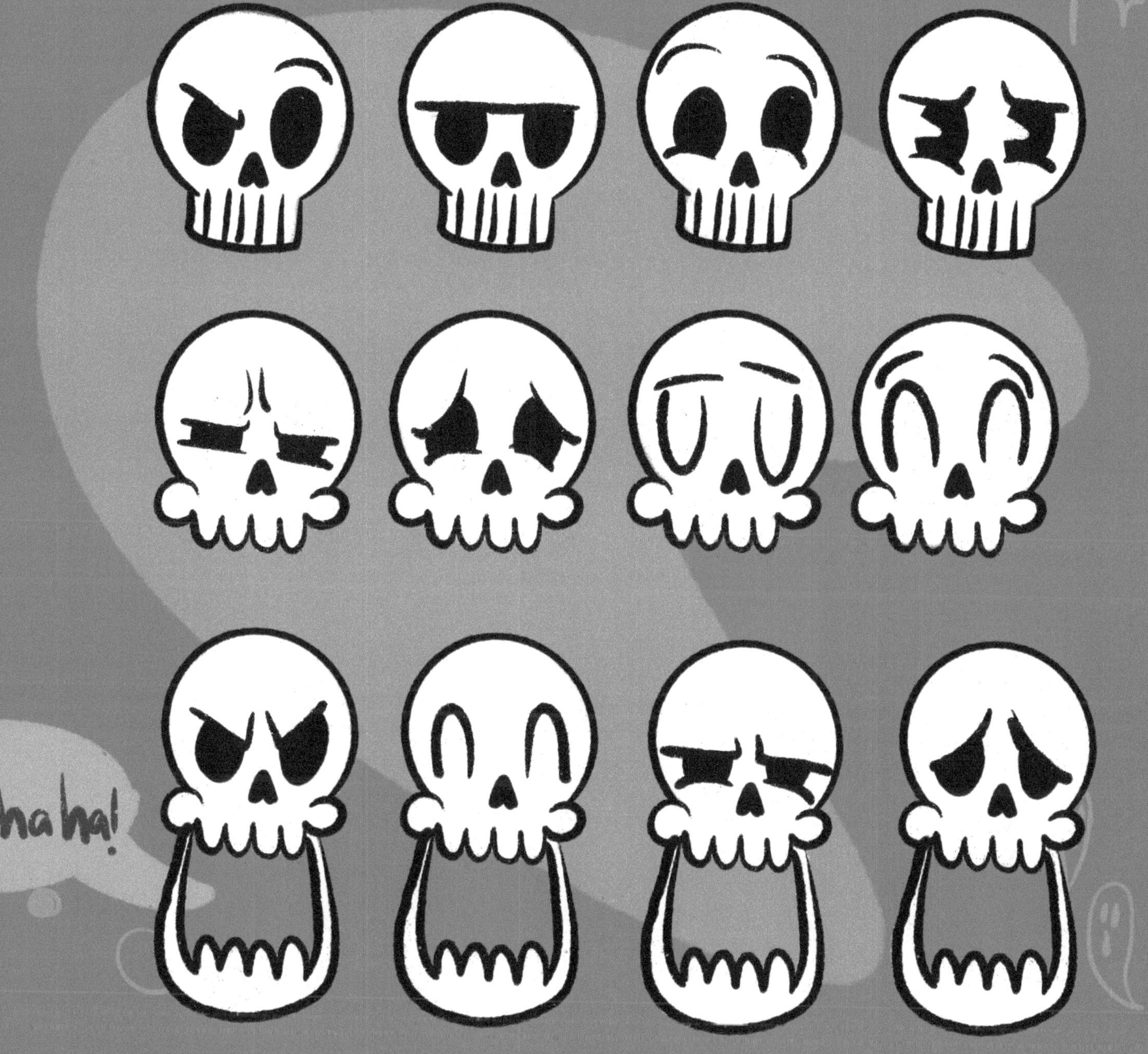

Witch

Sweet Witch

Broom Sticks and Spell Books

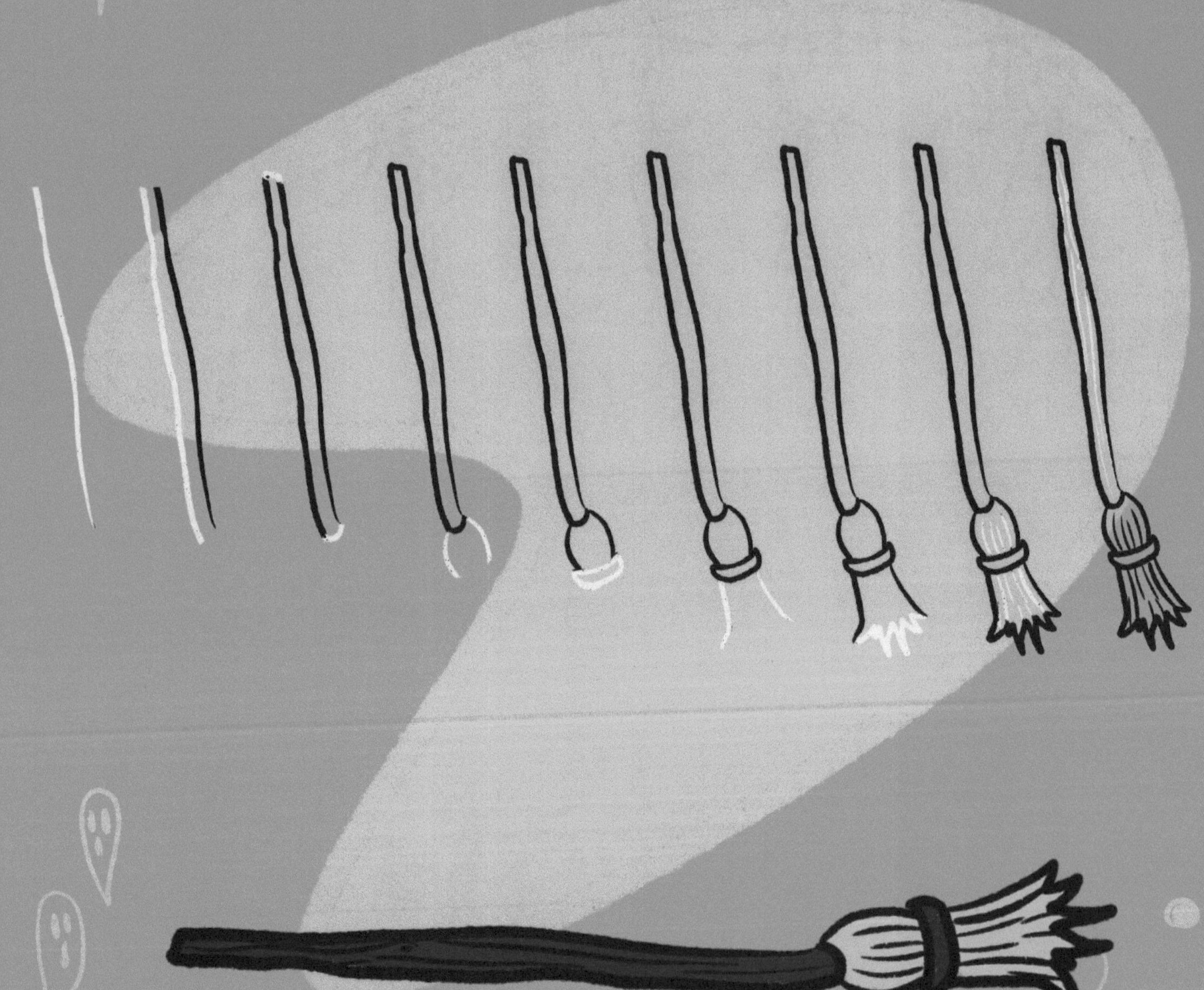

Spooky Paintings

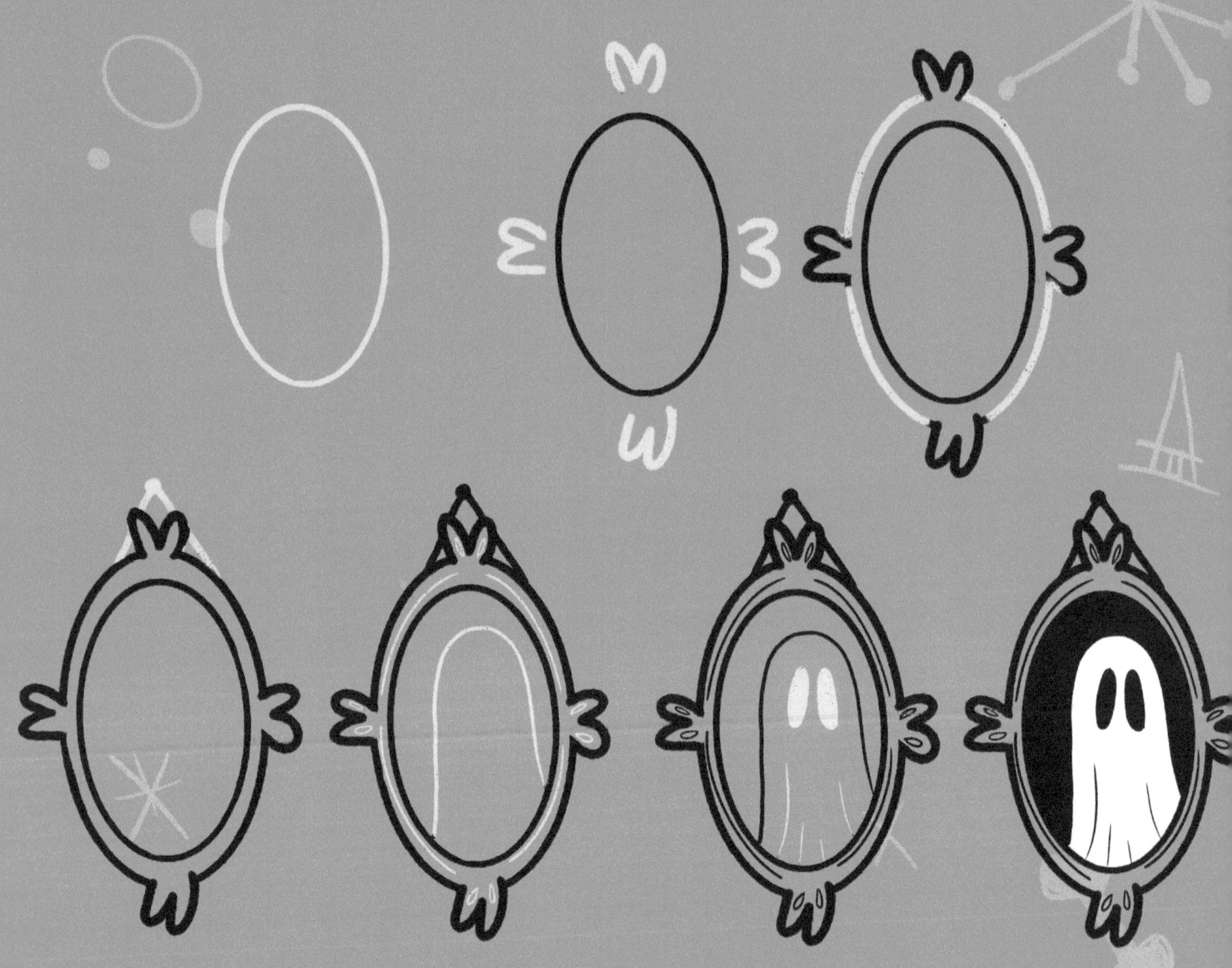

Spooky Paintings

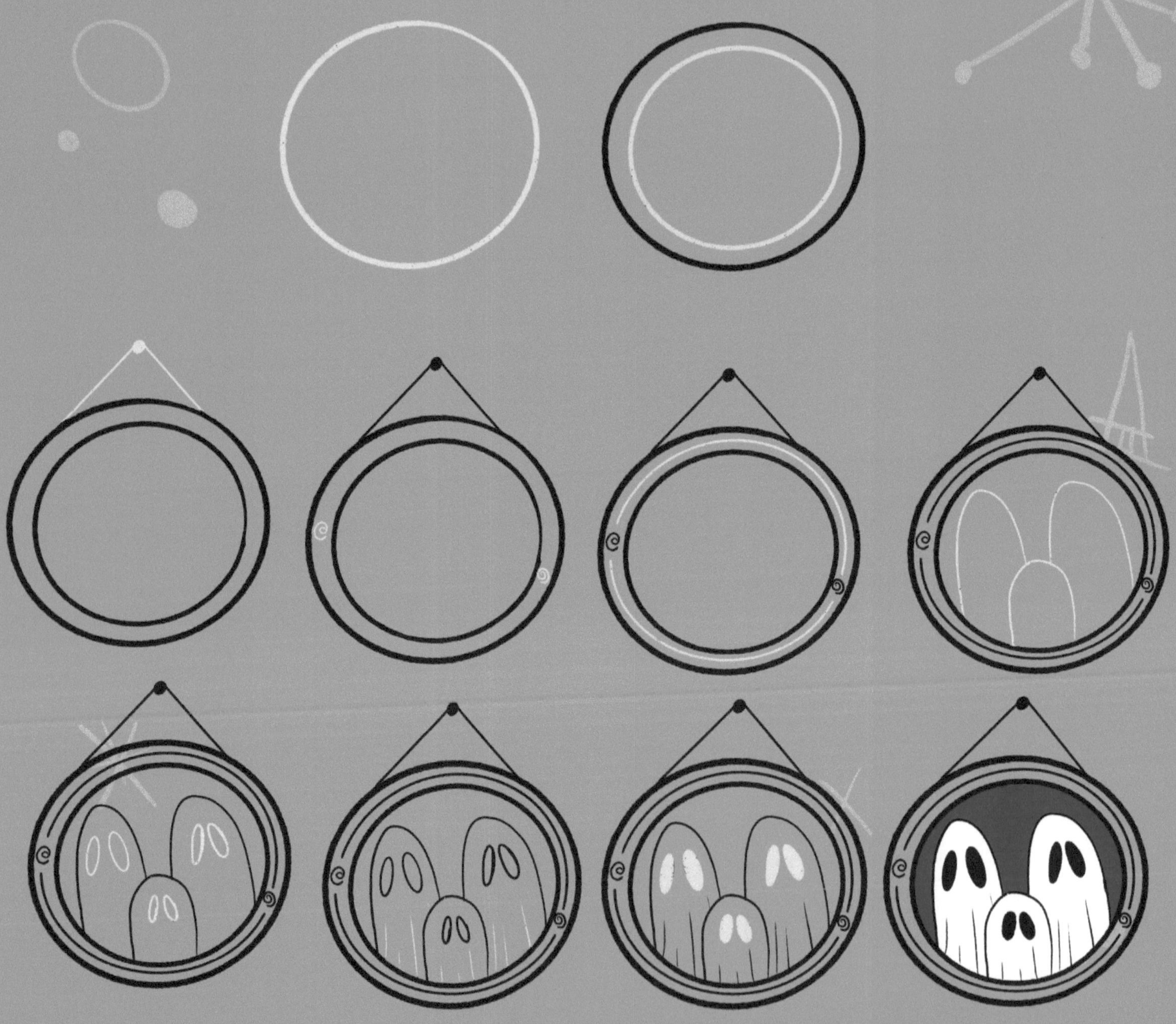

Spooky Plants

Spooky Plants

Thorny Vines

Boo Blossom

Ghostly Faces

Spooky Graveyard

RIP

Bones

Pigeon Hallows Crow

Spooky Sign

Dracula

Coffin

Spooky tree

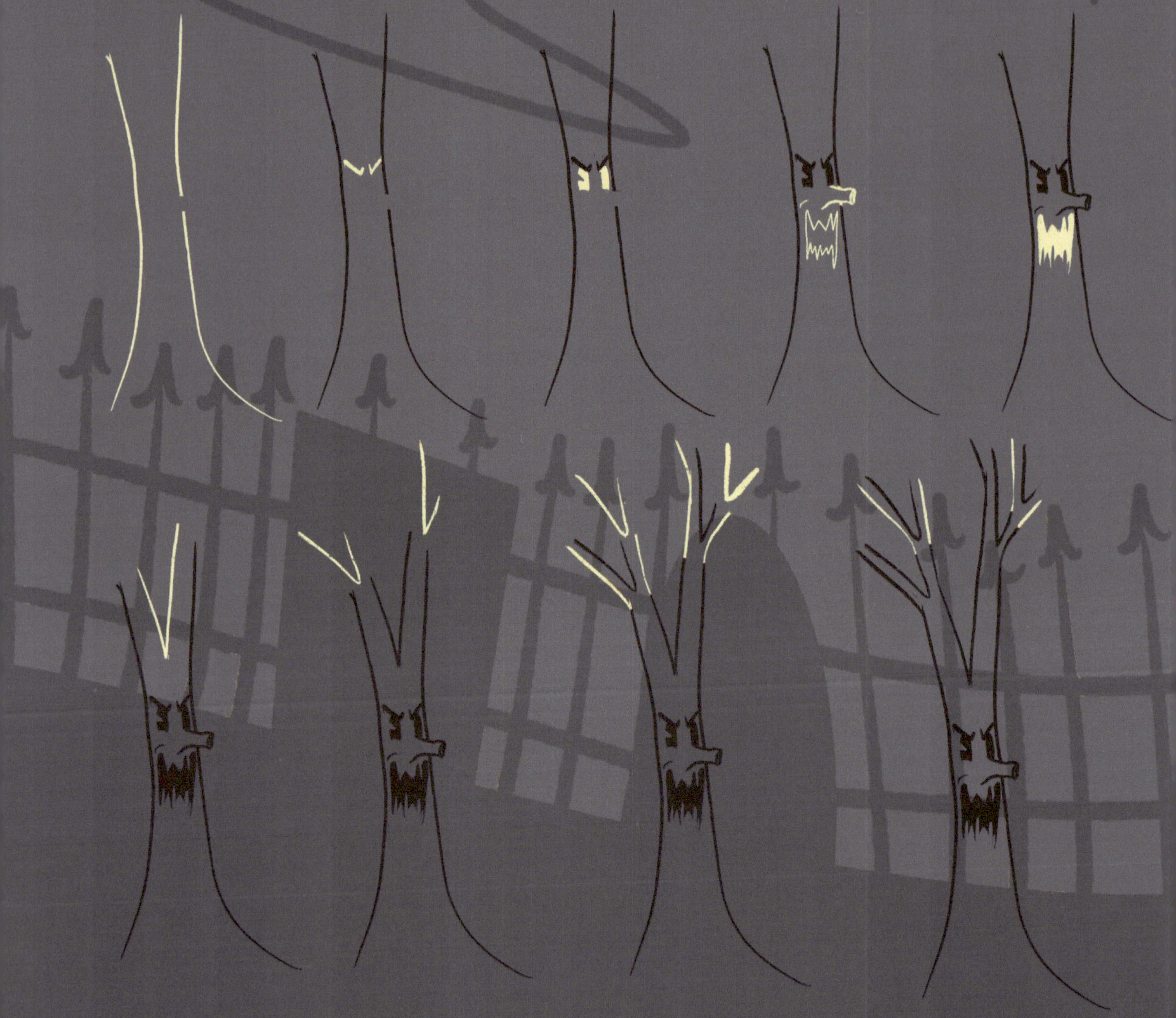

Spider webs

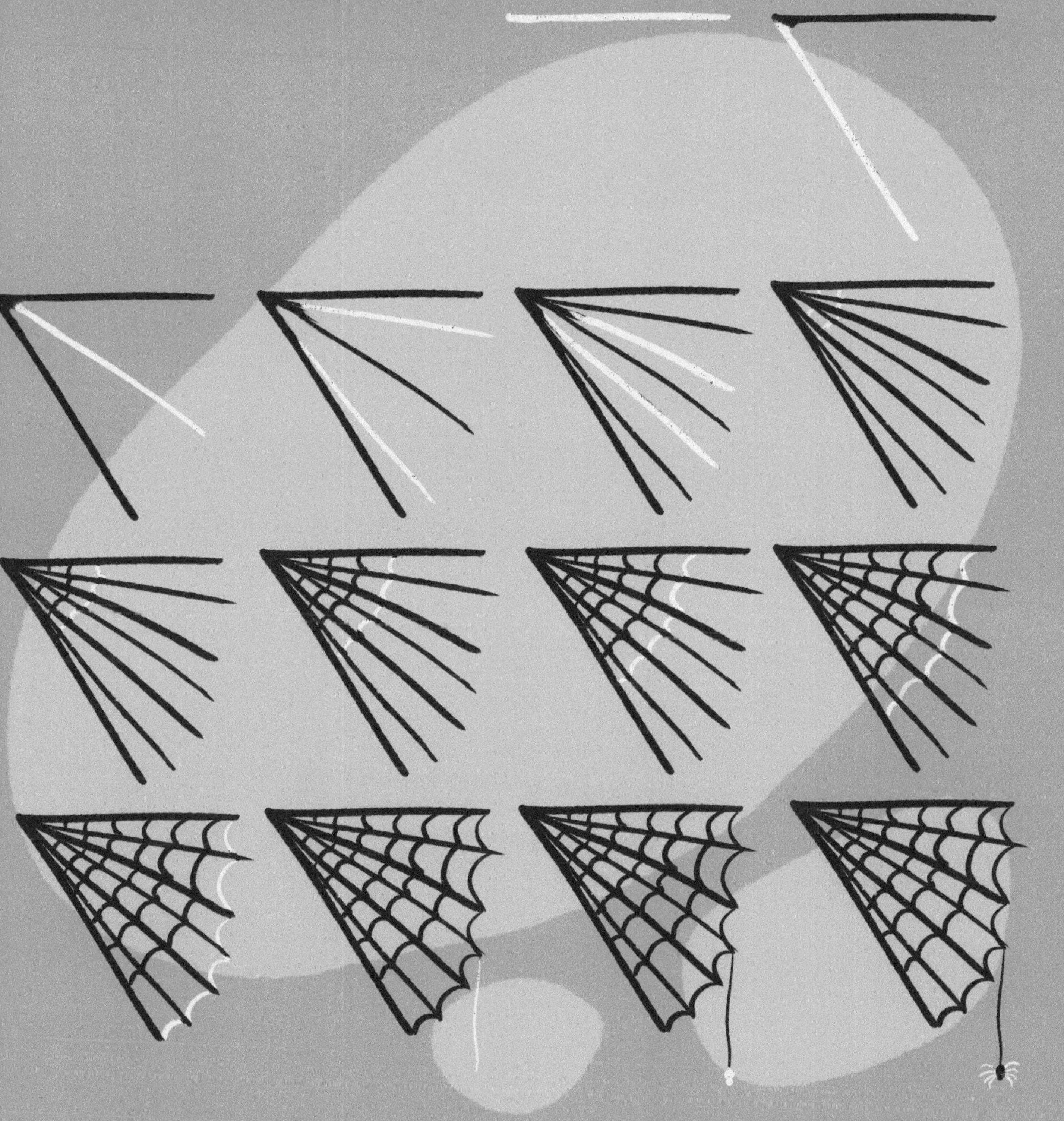

Bats

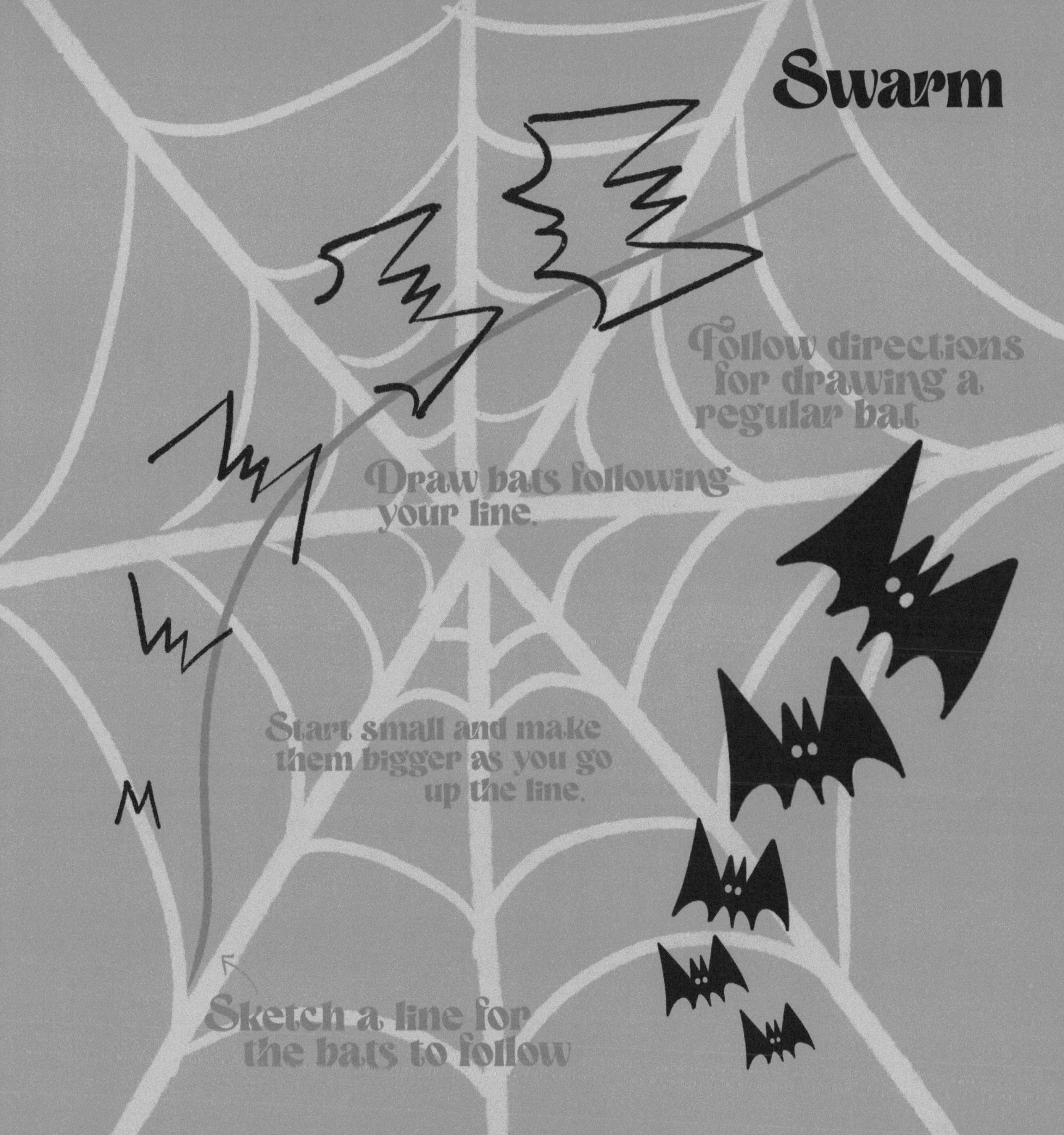

Swarm
Follow directions for drawing a regular bat
Draw bats following your line.
Start small and make them bigger as you go up the line.
Sketch a line for the bats to follow

Batty

Spooky Potions

Spooky Potions

Spooky Potions

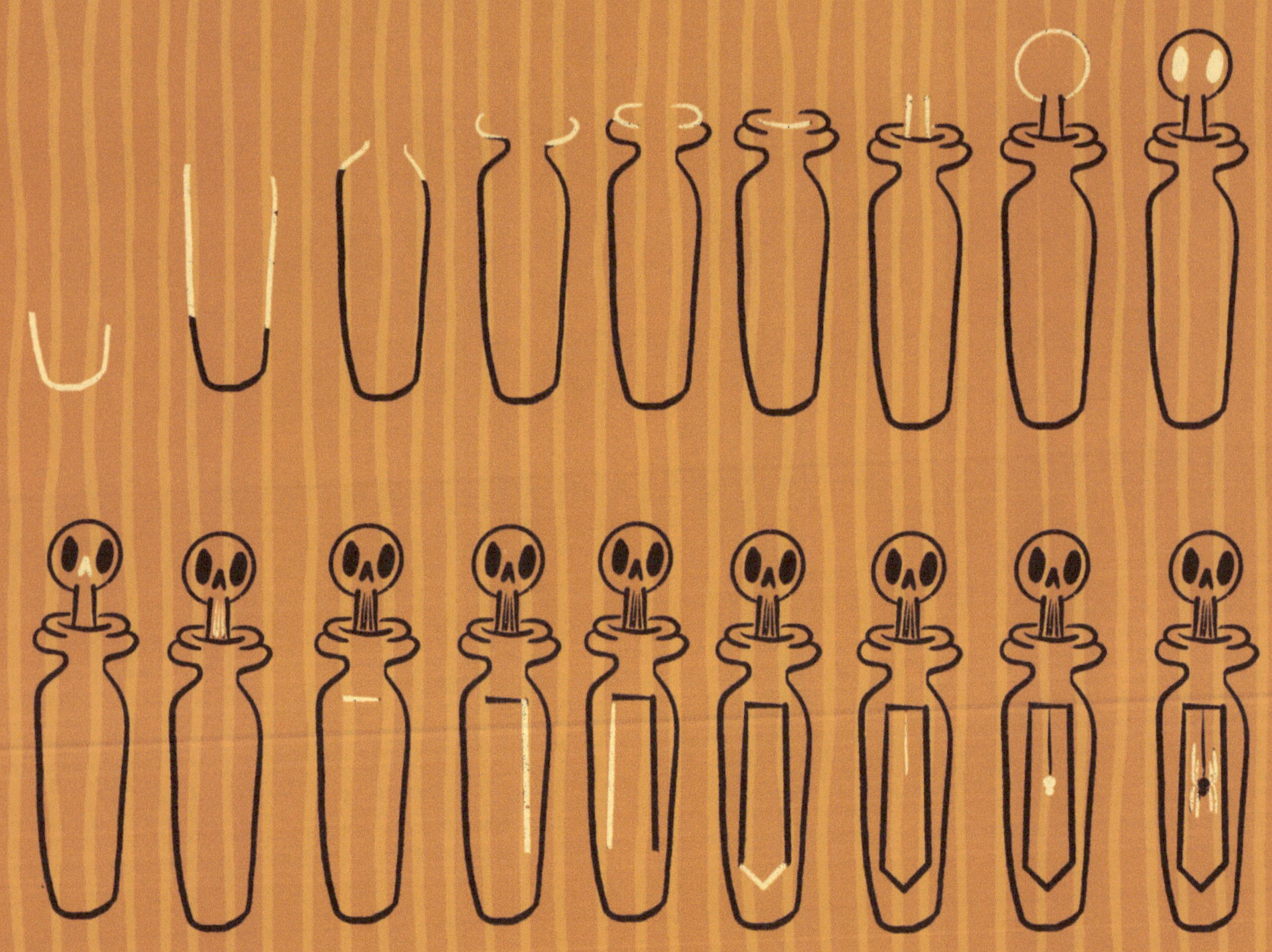

Other titles by Rebecca Demos

Pigeon Hallows
a coloring adventure

So I can draw
this thing...

Opposite Oppostand

So I can draw
this thing...

written & illustrated by
Rebecca Demos

about the
author & illustrator

Rebecca Demos has been teaching art for the past ten years and illustrating books for the past three. She lives in Arlington Heights with her two daughter's Mae & Molly and her best friend and husband Chris.

@BHillgie

Find her on Instagram and other works using the we code.

www.ingramcontent.com/pod-product-compliance
Lightning Source LLC
Chambersburg PA
CBHW040135240726
48664CB00002B/494